Sanjeev Kapoor's

Vegetarian
Breakfasts

Sanjeev Kapoor's

Vegetarian

Breakfasts

In association with Alyona Kapoor

Popular
prakashan

www.popularprakashan.com

POPULAR PRAKASHAN PVT. LTD.
301, Mahalaxmi Chambers
22, Bhulabhai Desai Road
Mumbai - 400026

(4080)
ISBN 13: 978-81-7991-332-1

Photography: Bharat Bhirangi

Published by Ramdas Bhatkal
for Popular Prakashan Pvt. Ltd.
301, Mahalaxmi Chambers
22, Bhulabhai Desai Road
Mumbai - 400026

"All happiness depends on a leisurely breakfast."

— John Gunther

Author's Note

In these hectic times, not many of us pay heed to what our mothers used to say every morning, as they piled one more buttered toast or one more dollop of upma onto our plates: "Eat up! You need a good breakfast to keep you going through the day!" They knew what nutritionists now tell us: that breakfast gives one the perfect start to a busy day; the right kind of fuel to power us through the hurly burly of our frenzied lives.

Today our busy schedules and some mistaken notions on weight loss have lead us to skip breakfast completely or to grab a frugal bite on the run. Most city dwellers regularly break their all-night fasts with a piece of fruit, or a cup of coffee or tea, or perhaps a glass of milk, or a greasy snack picked up from a street food stall. Which flies in the face of commonsense and basic human instinct that tell us that after a whole night's fasting, the body is ready to absorb nutrition which will help it to function efficiently through the rest of the day.

Several studies have proved that people who eat a good breakfast tend to be healthier with a lower body weight. Skipping breakfast leads to indiscriminate snacking to satisfy hunger pangs, with disastrous effects on the waistline and the weighing scale!

An ideal breakfast would comprise a serving of cereal, preferably whole grain, some dairy protein such as milk or yogurt, and a piece of fruit. Some power bowls manage to combine all three and I have included a few recipes for you. I have also included a whole range of vegetarian breakfast options that will keep you energetic and lively throughout the day.

Remember the old adage, *"Eat breakfast like a king, lunch like a prince, and dinner like a pauper."*

Happy Cooking!

Acknowledgements

Afsheen Panjwani
Anand Bhandiwad
Anil Bhandari
Anupa Das
Bharati Anand
Bhartendu Sharma
Drs. Meena and Ram Prabhoo
Gajendra Mule
Ganesh Pednekar
Harpal Singh Sokhi
Jayadeep Chaubal
Jyotsna and Mayur Dvivedi
Kalpana Deshmukh
Lohana Khaandaan
Mahendra Ghanekar

Manasi Morajkar
Mrs. Lata Lohana and
Capt. K. K. Lohana
Namrata and Sanjiv Bahl
Neelima Acharya
Neena Murdeshwar
Pooja and Rajeev Kapoor
Rajeev Matta
Rita D'Souza
Rutika Samtani
Saurabh Mishra
Smeeta Bhatkal
Tripta Bhagattjee
Trupti Kale
Vinayak Gawande

Contents

INDIAN BREAKFASTS

Corn Handvo

1 cup crushed sweet corn kernels

1 cup rice

½ cup split pigeon peas (*arhar dal/toovar dal*)

¼ cup split green gram (*dhuli moong dal*)

2 tablespoons split Bengal gram (*chana dal*)

2 tablespoons split black gram (*dhuli urad dal*)

½ cup sour yogurt

2 teaspoons soda bicarbonate

salt to taste

4 teaspoons sugar

2 teaspoons red chilli powder

¼ teaspoon turmeric powder

1 large onion, chopped

2 tablespoons chopped fresh coriander leaves

2-3 green chillies, chopped

4 tablespoons oil

2 dried red chillies, broken in half

1 bay leaf

a pinch of asafoetida (*hing*)

1 teaspoon mustard seeds

1 tablespoon lemon juice

- Soak the rice with all the *dals* in five cups of water for two hours. Drain. Grind to a coarse paste and add enough water to make a batter of moderately thick consistency. Mix in the yogurt and a teaspoon of soda bicarbonate. Cover batter and leave in a dark place for two or three hours to ferment.

- Add the corn, salt, sugar, chilli powder, turmeric powder, onion, coriander leaves and green chillies to the batter and mix well.

- Preheat the oven to 200°C.

- Heat the oil in a pan; add the red chillies, bay leaf, asafoetida and mustard seeds.

- Sprinkle the remaining soda bicarbonate over the batter and pour in the lemon juice. Immediately pour the hot seasoning over the batter and whisk briskly to mix.

- Grease a baking tray. Pour the batter into it till half full.

- Pour some water into a slightly larger baking tray and place the tray with the batter in it. Bake for twenty to twenty-five minutes.

- Cut into wedges and serve hot.

Achari Idils

35-40 mini *idlis*

2 tablespoons refined mustard oil

4 dried red chillies

½ teaspoon mustard seeds

¼ teaspoon fenugreek seeds (*methi dana*)

¾ teaspoon cumin seeds

½ teaspoon fennel seeds (*saunf*)

½ teaspoon onion seeds (*kalonji*)

salt to taste

2 tablespoons chopped fresh coriander leaves

- Heat the mustard oil to smoking point and set aside to cool.

- Dry-roast the red chillies, mustard seeds, fenugreek seeds, cumin seeds, fennel seeds and onion seeds till fragrant. Grind to a powder, add salt and mix with the cooled oil.

- Place the ground spices in a pan and heat gently. Add the *idlis* and toss well to mix. Serve hot, garnished with coriander leaves.

Chef's Tip

If mini *idlis* are not available, you can cut regular *idlis* into quarters for this recipe.

Bajre Ki Roti With Banana Stuffing

Dough

¾ cup *bajra* flour

¼ cup refined flour (*maida*)

salt to taste

1 tablespoon oil +
   for shallow-frying

roasted sesame seeds (*til*)

Stuffing

3 unripe Rajeri bananas

salt to taste

2 teaspoons green chilli paste

1 teaspoon sugar

2 teaspoons lemon juice

1 tablespoon fresh coriander
   leaves, chopped

- To make the stuffing, steam the unpeeled bananas; peel and mash while still hot. Add salt, the green chilli paste, sugar, lemon juice and coriander leaves. Mix well till smooth.

- To make the dough, put the *bajra* flour, refined flour and salt into a bowl and mix well. Add one tablespoon of oil and enough water and knead into a soft dough. Divide into eight equal *pedas*.

- Sprinkle some refined flour on the worktop, place a *peda* on it and gently spread it out with your fingers, making sure that the outer edges are thinner

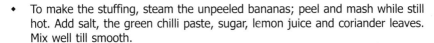

19

than the centre. Place a portion of the stuffing in the centre and gather the edges together and roll out once again into a *peda*.

• Lightly press one side of the *peda* into the roasted sesame seeds. Roll in refined flour and gently flatten the *peda* with your fingers to make as thin a *roti* as you can. You need not use a rolling pin.

• Heat a *tawa* and place the *roti* on it. When one side is lightly browned, turn over and cook the other side. Drizzle some oil all around and continue to cook till both sides are light golden brown.

• Serve hot.

Chef's Tip:
Refined flour is used in the dough because it helps to bind the *bajra* flour into a dough.

Sooji Kheer

½ cup semolina (*rawa/sooji*)
1½ litres skimmed milk
7-8 threads of saffron
½ cup sugar

2 tablespoons *charoli (chironji)*
20 almonds, blanched and slivered

- Roast the semolina in a thick-bottomed pan over low heat for fifteen minutes or till light brown.
- Soak the saffron in one tablespoon of milk.
- Bring the remaining milk to a boil, lower heat and simmer till reduced to one litre.
- Add the reduced milk to the *rawa*, stirring continuously to prevent lumps from forming.
- Cook over high heat till the mixture comes to a boil. Add the sugar and simmer for two or three minutes. Add the saffron and stir well.
- Garnish with the *charoli* and almond slivers and serve hot or cold.

Cheese And Coriander Parantha

1 cup grated processed cheese

½ cup chopped fresh coriander leaves

1¾ cups wholewheat flour (*atta*) + for dusting

salt to taste

milk as required

1 inch ginger, chopped

2 green chillies, chopped

2 teaspoons *chaat masala*

oil/ghee for shallow-frying

- Place the wholewheat flour and salt in a bowl. Add the coriander leaves and enough milk and knead into a soft dough. Cover the dough with a damp cloth and rest it for twenty to twenty-five minutes. Divide the dough into eight equal portions and shape into balls.

- Mix together the cheese, ginger, green chillies and *chaat masala*. Divide the mixture into eight equal portions.

- Roll out each ball of dough into a medium-sized *chapatti*. Spread a portion of the cheese mixture over the *chapatti*. Fold the *chapatti* up like an envelope and roll out into square *paranthas.*

- Heat a *tawa*; place each *parantha* on it and shallow-fry, turning the *parantha* over and drizzling a little oil around till both sides are light golden and crisp.

- Cut into four and serve immediately.

Besan Omelettes With Sprout Filling

Omelette Batter

1½ cups gram flour (*besan*)

4 green chillies

1 teaspoon red chilli powder

¼ teaspoon turmeric powder

¼ teaspoon carom seeds (*ajwain*)

3 tablespoons yogurt

1 tablespoon chopped fresh coriander leaves

salt to taste

oil for shallow-frying

butter, to serve

Filling

1 cup sprouted *moong*, blanched

1 tablespoon oil

2 medium onions, chopped

2 medium tomatoes, seeded and chopped

2 green chillies, chopped

¼ teaspoon turmeric powder

½ teaspoon red chilli powder

½ teaspoon *chaat masala*

salt to taste

1 teaspoon lemon juice

1 tablespoon chopped fresh coriander leaves

- For the omelette batter, mix together the gram flour, green chillies, chilli powder, turmeric powder, carom seeds, yogurt, coriander leaves and salt. Add one and one-fourth cup of water and whisk to a smooth batter of pouring consistency. Rest the batter for about fifteen minutes.

- To make the filling, heat the oil in a pan; add the onions and tomatoes and sauté for two minutes.

- Add the green chillies and sprouts and continue to sauté for half a minute. Add the turmeric powder, chilli powder, *chaat masala*, salt, lemon juice and coriander leaves and sauté for one minute. Remove from heat and set aside.

- Heat a *tawa*, grease it with a little oil and pour a little batter onto it. Spread into a thin round with the back of the ladle and cook till golden brown on both sides.

- Place some filling in the centre and roll up. Serve hot with a dollop of butter.

Bread Upma

6-8 slices day-old bread

4 tablespoons oil

a pinch of asafoetida (*hing*)

½ teaspoon cumin seeds

¼ teaspoon mustard seeds

1 medium onion, chopped

1 medium potato, boiled, peeled and cubed

¼ teaspoon turmeric powder

salt to taste

½ teaspoon red chilli powder

1 teaspoon lemon juice

2 green chillies, chopped

2 tablespoons chopped fresh coriander leaves

- Break the bread into smaller pieces.

- Heat the oil in a *kadai*; add a pinch of asafoetida, the cumin seeds and mustard seeds. When the cumin seeds change colour and mustard seeds begin to splutter, add the onion and sauté for a few minutes till translucent. Add the potato and sauté for two minutes.

- Add the turmeric powder, salt and bread and mix well; add the chilli powder and toss to mix. Sprinkle some water over the mixture and cook for two minutes. Add the lemon juice, green chillies and coriander leaves. Toss well to mix and serve hot.

Lasun And Rice Thepla

2 cups wholewheat flour (*atta*)

1 tablespoon garlic paste

2 tablespoons fresh green garlic, chopped (optional)

1 cup leftover cooked rice, mashed

½ teaspoon turmeric powder

1 teaspoon red chilli powder

salt to taste

2 tablespoons chopped fresh coriander leaves

4 tablespoons oil + for shallow-frying

- Place the wholewheat flour, garlic paste, green garlic, mashed rice, turmeric powder, chilli powder, salt and coriander leaves in a bowl.
- Mix in four tablespoons of oil and knead with enough water into a medium soft dough.
- Divide into twelve portions and roll each one out thinly into five-inch round *theplas*.
- Heat a *tawa* and cook the *theplas* on both sides, drizzling a little oil around.
- Serve hot with pickle or yogurt.

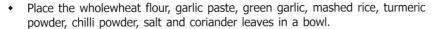

27

Mixed Flour Onion Cheela

2 cups rice flour

¼ cup wholewheat flour (*atta*)

2-3 spring onions, chopped

6-7 spring onion green stalks, chopped

¾ teaspoon ginger paste

2 green chillies, chopped

¾ teaspoon cumin seeds

salt to taste

oil for shallow-frying

- Mix together the rice flour and wholewheat flour in a bowl. Add enough water to make a smooth batter of pouring consistency. Leave to rest for half an hour.

- Add the spring onions, spring onion greens, ginger paste, green chillies, cumin seeds and salt to taste and mix well.

- Heat a *tawa* and lightly grease it. When moderately hot, wipe it clean with a cloth.

- Pour one ladleful of batter on the *tawa* and spread it with the back of the ladle as thinly as possible into a round pancake.

- Cook for a while and flip it over. Drizzle oil around and cook on both sides till golden brown. Serve hot with chutney or tomato ketchup.

Dal Pakwan

Dal

1 cup split Bengal gram (*chana dal*)

salt to taste

¼ teaspoon turmeric powder

½ teaspoon red chilli powder

¼ teaspoon *garam masala* powder

¾ teaspoon dried mango powder (*amchur*)

3 tablespoons oil

1 teaspoon cumin seeds

4-5 green chillies, slit

8-10 curry leaves

1 medium onion, chopped

½ cup chopped fresh coriander leaves

Pakwan

1 cup refined flour (*maida*)

2 tablespoons wholewheat flour (*atta*)

1 tablespoon semolina (*rawa/sooji*)

¼ teaspoon cumin seeds

10-12 black peppercorns, crushed

5 tablespoons hot oil + for deep-frying

salt to taste

- Soak the *chana dal* in three cups of water for about one hour. Drain and boil with three cups of water, salt and turmeric powder till just done.

- Heat a pan; add the boiled *dal* and half a cup of water if the *dal* is too dry. Stir and add half the chilli powder, half the *garam masala* powder, the dried mango powder and salt. Stir gently and cook over low heat.

- Heat the oil in a separate pan and add the cumin seeds. When they begin to change colour, add the green chillies, curry leaves, remaining *garam masala* powder and remaining chilli powder. Stir and pour over the *dal*, mix well and remove from heat.

- To make the *pakwan,* sift the refined flour and wholewheat flour into a large bowl. Add the semolina, cumin seeds, crushed peppercorns, five tablespoons of hot oil and salt. Add enough water and knead into a medium-soft dough.

- Divide the dough into eight portions and roll each portion out into a four-inch round *chapatti.* Prick lightly with a fork.

- Heat the oil in a *kadai* and deep-fry the *pakwan* over low heat till golden and crisp. Drain on absorbent paper.

- Garnish the *dal* with onion and coriander leaves and serve hot with the *pakwan.*

Peethiwali Puri With Aloo Chana

Puris

1½ cups wholewheat flour (*atta*)

¼ cup split black gram (*dhuli urad dal*)

salt to taste

1 tablespoon oil + for deep-frying

3 tablespoons *ghee*

1 inch cinnamon

a pinch of asafoetida (*hing*)

1½ teaspoons cumin seeds

2 tablespoons coriander seed

1 teaspoon red chilli powder

salt to taste

Aloo Chana

1 cup chickpeas (*kabuli chana*)

2 medium potatoes, boiled, peeled and cubed

a pinch of soda bicarbonate

salt to taste

1 inch ginger

5 garlic cloves

3 green chillies

4 tablespoons *ghee*

3 medium onions, ground

1 teaspoon red chilli powder

1 cup tomato purée

2 tablespoons *chana masala*

2 tablespoons chopped fresh coriander leaves

- Soak the split black gram in one cup of water for two hours. Drain.

- Mix together the wholewheat flour, salt and one tablespoon of oil in a bowl. Add enough water and knead into a dough. Cover with a damp cloth and set aside for at least fifteen minutes.

- Heat the *ghee* in a pan; add the cinnamon, asafoetida, cumin seeds and coriander seeds and sauté for a while. Add the soaked gram and continue to sauté. Add the chilli powder and salt and mix well. Remove the cinnamon stick and set the mixture aside to cool.

- Divide the dough into twelve equal portions and roll into balls. Make a hollow in each ball, fill it with the filling, fold over and shape into a ball again. Press lightly on the work surface. Roll out or press by hand into *puris*.

- Heat the oil in a *kadai*; slide the *puris* gently into the oil and deep-fry till the *puris* puff up and are evenly fried on both the sides. Drain on absorbent paper and serve hot with *aloo chana*.

- To make the *aloo chana*, soak the chickpeas overnight. Drain, add three cups of water and cook in a pressure cooker with a pinch of soda bicarbonate and salt till soft.

- Grind the ginger, garlic and green chillies to a paste.

- Heat two tablespoons of *ghee* and sauté the ground onion till pink. Add the ginger-garlic-green chilli paste and red chilli powder and continue to sauté till fragrant. Add the tomato purée and sauté till the *ghee* separates. Add the boiled *chana* along with the water and simmer for five minutes.

- Take the pan off the heat and sprinkle *chana masala* over. Heat the remaining *ghee* till smoking hot and stir into the *chana*. Cover the pan and leave to stand for five minutes. Garnish with coriander leaves and serve hot with *peethiwali puris*.

Pineapple Sheera

1 small (¼ kilogram) pineapple, peeled and chopped

1 cup semolina (*rawa/sooji*)

1 cup *ghee*

a pinch of saffron

1 cup sugar

5-6 cashew nuts

5-6 almonds

- Heat the *ghee* in a pan; add the semolina and cook, stirring continuously, till golden brown. Add the saffron and mix.
- Add the pineapple and cook for another two or three minutes.
- Stir in two cups of water; cover and cook over medium heat for three minutes.
- Add the sugar and keep stirring till all the moisture evaporates and the semolina is cooked completely.
- Garnish with cashew nuts and almonds and serve hot.

Protein Rich Poha

2 cups pressed rice flakes
(*poha*)

½ cup sprouted brown gram,
(*matki*) blanched

2 tablespoons oil

½ teaspoon cumin seeds

1 inch ginger, grated

3 green chillies, halved

6-8 curry leaves

2 medium onions, chopped

½ teaspoon turmeric powder

salt to taste

1 tablespoon lemon juice

2 tablespoons chopped fresh
coriander leaves

- Place the *poha* in a colander and pour three to four cups of water over to moisten the rice flakes. Drain and set aside.

- Heat the oil in a non-stick pan and add the cumin seeds. When they begin to change colour, add the ginger, green chillies, curry leaves, onions, turmeric powder and *matki* and sauté for five to seven minutes, till the onions soften.

- Add the *poha* and toss over medium heat till heated through. Add the salt and lemon juice and toss well.

- Serve at once, garnished with coriander leaves.

Missal Pav

1 cup sprouted green gram
(*moong*)

1 cup sprouted brown gram
(*matki*)

2 tablespoons oil

a pinch of asafoetida (*hing*)

½ teaspoon mustard seeds

a few curry leaves

2 large onions, finely chopped

2 green chillies, slit

1 teaspoon garlic paste

1 teaspoon ginger paste

½ teaspoon turmeric powder

1½ teaspoons red chilli powder

1 teaspoon coriander-cumin
powder

salt to taste

1 teaspoon *garam masala*
powder

2 tablespoons fresh coriander
leaves, finely chopped

½ cup *farsan*

lemon juice

lemon slices

8 *pav*

- Mix both the sprouted gram in a colander and wash under running water for one minute. Drain.

- Heat the oil in a pan; add the asafoetida, mustard seeds, curry leaves and half the onions. Sauté for one minute and add the green chillies, garlic paste and ginger paste. Stir well and sprinkle a little water.

- Add the turmeric powder, red chilli powder and coriander-cumin powder. Mix well and add the sprouted gram. Add salt to taste and three cups of water and bring to a boil.

- Add the *garam masala* powder and coriander leaves, reserving some for garnishing Cover and cook for ten to twelve minutes.

- To serve, pour a ladleful of cooked sprouted gram into a deep bowl. Sprinkle generously with *farsan*. Sprinkle the remaining onion, remaining coriander leaves and freshly squeezed lemon juice over the *farsan*.

- Serve with lemon slices and *pav*.

Sabudana Thalipeeth

1 cup sago (*sabudana*), soaked

2 medium potatoes, boiled, peeled and mashed

2-3 green chillies, chopped

¼ teaspoon red chilli powder

½ cup crushed roasted peanuts

2 tablespoons chopped fresh coriander leaves

1 tablespoon cumin seeds

salt to taste

4-5 teaspoons *ghee*

- Mix together the *sabudana*, mashed potatoes, green chillies, chilli powder, roasted peanuts, coriander leaves, cumin seeds and salt.

- Divide the mixture into four portions and form each portion into a ball.

- Grease a thick plastic or polythene sheet with a little oil and place the *sabudana* ball on it. Flatten the ball with moistened or greased fingers into a thick round.

- Heat a *tawa* and add a teaspoon of *ghee*. Transfer the *thalipeeth* to the *tawa* by gently turning the *thalipeeth* out onto the tawa and peeling the plastic off. Cook, spreading both sides with *ghee* till light golden brown.

- Serve hot with chutney.

Palak Puri With Tamatar Aloo

Puris

1½ cups wholewheat flour (*atta*)

15-20 large spinach leaves (*palak*), blanched and puréed

salt to taste

1 tablespoon oil + for deep-frying

Tamatar Aloo

2 large tomatoes, chopped

4 medium unpeeled potatoes, diced

2 tablespoons oil

1 teaspoon cumin seeds

1 inch ginger, chopped

½ teaspoon turmeric powder

1 teaspoon coriander powder

½ teaspoon cumin powder

1 teaspoon red chilli powder

salt to taste

- Mix the *palak* purée with the wholewheat flour; add salt and one tablespoon of oil and knead into a moderately firm dough. Cover the dough with a damp cloth and leave to rest for about ten minutes.

- To make the *tamatar aloo*, heat the oil in a pan; add the cumin seeds and tomatoes and sauté for a few minutes. Add the ginger and continue to sauté for a while.

- Add the potatoes, turmeric powder, coriander powder, cumin powder, chilli powder and salt. Stir to mix and add two-and-a-half cups of water. Cover and cook over low heat till the potatoes are done.

- Divide the dough into sixteen equal balls (*pedas*) and roll into four-inch round *puris*. Heat the oil in a *kadai* and deep-fry the *puris* over medium heat. Drain on absorbent paper and serve hot with *tamatar aloo*.

Vegetable Rawa Upma

1½ cups semolina (*rawa/sooji*)

1 medium carrot, cut into ¼-inch cubes

6-8 French beans, cut into ¼-inch pieces

1 medium cauliflower, separated into small florets

¼ cup shelled green peas

1 medium green capsicum, cut into ¼-inch pieces

salt to taste

5 tablespoons oil

½ teaspoon mustard seeds

2 dried red chillies, broken in half

2 teaspoons split black gram (*dhuli urad dal*)

10-12 curry leaves

4 green chillies, chopped

1 medium onion, chopped

1 inch ginger, chopped

a pinch asafoetida (*hing*)

1 tablespoon lemon juice

- Dry-roast the semolina in a *kadai* without allowing it to brown. Set aside to cool.

- Bring four cups of water to a boil in a deep pan; add a little salt, the carrot, beans, cauliflower and green peas and cook for six to eight minutes, or till the vegetables are almost done. Drain the vegetables and set aside.

- Heat the oil in a *kadai*; add the mustard seeds and when they begin to splutter, add the red chillies, split black gram, curry leaves and green chillies. Mix well.

- Add the onion, ginger and capsicum and continue to cook over high heat for two minutes. Add the cooked vegetables and sprinkle with asafoetida and salt to taste.

- Pour in four or five cups of hot water and bring the mixture to a boil. Add the roasted semolina and cook, stirring continuously, to prevent lumps from forming. Cook for three to four minutes, or until all the water has been absorbed.

- Stir in the lemon juice and serve hot.

Paruppu Vadas With Ginger Tomato Chutney

1½ cups split Bengal gram (*chana dal*)

½ cup split pigeon peas (*arhar dal/toovar dal*)

½ cup split black gram (*dhuli urad dal*)

¼ teaspoon asafoetida (*hing*)

3 green chillies, chopped

2 medium onions, chopped

½ inch ginger, chopped

2 tablespoons chopped fresh coriander leaves

salt to taste

a pinch of soda bicarbonate

2 tablespoons oil + for deep-frying

Chutney

1 inch ginger, chopped

2 large ripe red tomatoes, chopped

1 teaspoon oil

1 small onion, chopped

½ tablespoon sesame seeds *(til)*, roasted and powdered

½ tablespoon peanuts, roasted and powdered

½ teaspoon cumin seeds, powdered

1 teaspoon red chilli powder

½ tablespoon grated jaggery

salt to taste

- Soak all the *dals* together for three or four hours. Drain.

- Add the asafoetida and green chillies to the soaked *dals* and grind to a coarse paste.

- Add the onions, ginger paste, coriander leaves, salt and soda bicarbonate and mix well. Heat two tablespoons of oil and stir it into the batter. Do not add any water to the batter.

- Place a spoonful of batter on a clean plastic or polythene sheet and pat into the shape of a *vada*.

- Heat the oil in a *kadai* and deep-fry the *vadas* till crisp. Drain on absorbent paper and serve hot with ginger tomato chutney.

- To make the chutney, heat the oil in a pan. Add the tomatoes, ginger and onion and cook over medium heat till brown and pulpy. This may take around twenty minutes. Set aside to cool.

- Add the sesame seeds, peanuts, cumin seed powder, chilli powder, jaggery and salt to the cooled tomato mixture and grind to a smooth paste. Store in an airtight bottle till ready to serve.

Makai Aur Methi Parantha

2 cups wholewheat flour (*atta*)

salt to taste

½ cup sweet corn kernels, crushed

1 cup chopped fresh fenugreek leaves (*methi*)

½ cup yogurt

1 tablespoon oil + for shallow-frying

3 medium potatoes, boiled, peeled and mashed

salt to taste

3-4 green chillies, chopped

- Add salt to the wholewheat flour and mix. Add the yogurt, fenugreek leaves, one tablespoon of oil and knead with three-fourth cup of water into a dough.

- In a separate bowl, mix together the mashed potatoes, crushed corn, salt and green chillies. Divide the dough and filling into eight equal portions.

- Roll out each portion of the dough into a small *puri*. Place a portion of filling in the centre, gather the edges and pinch them together and roll into a ball. Cover the dough with a damp cloth and leave to rest for about fifteen minutes.

- Heat a *tawa*. Press the stuffed balls down lightly, sprinkle with a little flour and roll out into fairly thick *paranthas*.

- Shake off the excess flour and roast on a *tawa* over high heat. Drizzle a little oil around and cook till golden. Flip over and drizzle some more oil around and cook till the other side is golden. Serve hot.

Sada Dosa With Coconut Chutney

INDIAN BREAKFASTS

Dosa

2¾ cups parboiled rice
(*ukda chawal*)

¼ cup rice

1 cup split black gram
(*dhuli urad dal*)

1 teaspoon fenugreek seeds
(*methi dana*), optional

salt to taste

oil for shallow-frying

Coconut Chutney

1 cup grated fresh coconut

salt to taste

2 tablespoons oil

2 dried red chillies, broken into
3 pieces each

¼ teaspoon mustard seeds

½ teaspoon split black gram
(*dhuli urad dal*)

a large pinch of asafoetida (hing)

10-12 curry leaves

- Soak both the varieties of rice in six cups of water for at least four hours. Soak the split black gram with fenugreek seeds in three cups of water also for at least four hours.

- Drain and grind the rice and split gram separately into smooth batters of dropping consistency. Add salt and mix both the batters together thoroughly by hand in a whipping motion.

- Pour the batter into a large bowl or container, cover with a tight-fitting lid and leave the batter to stand overnight, or for about four to six hours, at room temperature to ferment.

- Heat a flat *tawa* (preferably non-stick) and grease with a little oil. Pour a ladleful of batter on it and spread as thinly as possible with the back of the ladle. Drizzle a little oil around the *dosa* and cook till crisp around the edges and golden brown. Fold over and remove. You can make about twenty to twenty-four *dosas*.

- To make the coconut chutney, use only the white part of the grated coconut. Grind the coconut with very little water. Add salt to taste and mix well. The consistency of the chutney should be thick.

- Heat the oil in a small pan; add the red chillies, mustard seeds and split black gram. When the mustard seeds begin to splutter and the gram turns a light brown, add the asafoetida and curry leaves.

- Add the seasoning to the coconut chutney and mix well. Serve with the *dosas*.

Chef's Tip
Do not get disheartened if the first couple of *dosas* go wrong; once the *tawa* gets seasoned, the rest of the *dosas* will turn out well.

Uttapam Sandwich

2¾ cups parboiled rice
(*ukda chawal*)

¼ cup rice

1 cup split black gram
(*dhuli urad dal*)

1 teaspoon fenugreek seeds
(*methi dana*), optional

salt to taste

½ cup butter

1 cup green coriander chutney

2 small onions, sliced

2 small tomatoes, sliced

2 small cucumbers, sliced

- Soak both the varieties of rice in six cups of water for at least four hours. Soak the split black gram with fenugreek seeds in three cups of water also for at least four hours.

- Drain and grind the rice and split gram separately into smooth batters of dropping consistency. Add salt and mix both the batters together thoroughly by hand in a whipping motion.

- Pour the batter into a large bowl or container, cover with a tight-fitting lid and leave the batter to stand overnight, or for about four to six hours, at room temperature to ferment.

- Transfer the batter to a separate bowl; add salt and enough water to get a consistency thicker than that for *dosas*.

- Heat a thick *tawa* or a non-stick pan. Add two drops of oil and wipe the *tawa* clean with a wet piece of muslin.

- Add a tablespoon of butter to the *tawa,* pour in half a ladleful of batter and spread it with the back of the ladle into a three-inch round. Pour as many uttapam as will fit on the *tawa*.

- Cook over low heat for three to five minutes. Flip the *uttapam* over and cook longer, if desired.

- Spread the coriander chutney on one side of each *uttapam.*

- Place a few slices of onion, tomato and cucumber over the chutney on half the *uttapams*.

- Place the rest of the *uttapams*, chutney side down over them. Press gently, cut into wedges and serve immediately.

Chef's Tip

You can also use ready-made *dosa* batter. Use three cups of the batter for this recipe.

Paushtik Bajre Ki Roti

1 cup millet (*bajra*) flour

¼ cup wholewheat flour (*atta*)

salt to taste

1 medium onion, grated

1 medium carrot, grated

2 green chillies, chopped

1 teaspoon carom seeds (*ajwain*)

- Sift the *bajra* flour, *atta* and salt together. Mix the flour mixture with the grated onion, grated carrot, chopped green chillies and *ajwain*. Add water, a little at a time, and knead the mixture into a medium soft dough. Do not over handle the dough.

- Divide the dough into eight equal portions and shape into balls (*pedas*). Wet your palms with water, take each portion of dough and pat it between your palms to make thin four or five-inch *rotis*.

- Heat a non-stick *tawa* and place the *roti* on it. Cook one side for about half a minute over medium heat; flip the *roti* over and cook the other side. Lower heat and cook both sides till the *bajra roti* is slightly browned.

- Serve hot.

Chef's Tip

It takes some practice, but you must try to make the rotis as thin as possible.

Masala Potato Uttapam

2¾ cups parboiled rice
(*ukda chawal*)

¼ cup rice

1 cup split black gram
(*dhuli urad dal*)

1 teaspoon fenugreek seeds
(*methi dana*),optional

salt to taste

oil for shallow-frying

4 teaspoons dry garlic chutney

Masala Potato

4 medium potatoes, boiled,
peeled and diced

2 tablespoons oil

½ teaspoon mustard seeds

2 teaspoons split black gram
(*dhuli urad dal*)

¼ teaspoon asafoetida (*hing*)

4 green chillies, chopped

10-12 curry leaves

2 medium onions, thinly sliced

1 inch ginger, grated

¼ teaspoon turmeric powder

1 tablespoon lemon juice

salt to taste

- Make the uttapam batter as on page 52.
- For the *masala* potato, heat the oil in a pan and add mustard seeds. When they begin to splutter, add the split black gram, asafoetida, green chillies and curry leaves. Stir and add the onions and fry till soft.

- Add the potatoes, ginger, turmeric powder, lemon juice and salt to taste. Toss well and remove from heat.

- Heat a non-stick *dosa* pan or frying pan, pour a ladleful of *uttapam* batter into it and spread with the back of the ladle into a four-inch round. Drizzle with oil and cook for a minute or two. Flip the *uttapam* and cook for a minute. Flip again and sprinkle with a little garlic chutney.

- Spread a portion of the *masala* potato over it, drizzle a few drops of oil all over and carefully turn the *uttapam* over. Leave to cook for one minute. Serve hot, *masala* side up.

Chef's Tip

You can also use ready-made *dosa* batter. Use three cups of the batter for this recipe.

Green Pea And Carrot Dalia

1 cup broken wheat (*dalia*)
½ cup shelled green peas
2 small carrots, diced
1 tablespoon oil
1 teaspoon cumin seeds
1 small onion, chopped

1 medium tomato, seeded and chopped
salt to taste
2 teaspoons butter
2 tablespoons chopped fresh coriander leaves

- Soak the *dalia* in two cups of water for thirty minutes. Drain.

- Heat the oil in a pressure cooker and add the cumin seeds. As they begin to change colour, add the onion and sauté till pink; add the green peas, carrots and tomato and sauté for one minute.

- Add the *dalia* and three cups of water; add salt to taste.

- Bring the mixture to a boil, fasten the lid of the pressure cooker and cook till the pressure is released twice (two whistles).

- Stir in the butter and coriander leaves and serve at once.

Spinach And Cheese Idlis

½ cup split black gram
  (*dhuli urad dal*)

1 cup *idli rawa*

salt to taste

8-10 spinach leaves

¼ cup grated cheese

½ teaspoon crushed black
  peppercorns

- Soak the *urad dal* and *idli rawa* separately for three or four hours. Drain and grind the *dal*, sprinkling water as required, to make a smooth, spongy batter.

- Drain the *idli rawa* and add it with the salt to the *dal* batter and mix thoroughly with your hands, using a whipping motion so that the batter is mixed well.

- Place the batter in a large pan or bowl, cover tightly and rest in a warm place for twenty-four hours, or at least overnight.

- Blanch the spinach leaves in boiling water for two or three minutes. Reserve a few leaves and purée the rest. Shred the reserved leaves.

- Add the spinach purée to the *idli* batter and mix well. Pour into lightly-oiled *idli* moulds, top with the shredded spinach leaves and grated cheese.

- Sprinkle crushed peppercorns and steam till the *idlis* are done.

- Serve the *idlis* with a spicy sauce.

Microwave Poha

2 cups thick rice flakes (*poha*)

3 medium onions, finely chopped

3-4 green chillies, slit and seeded

¼ cup roasted peanuts (optional), crushed

2 tablespoons oil

8-10 curry leaves

1 teaspoon turmeric powder

salt to taste

1 tablespoon lemon juice

a few sprigs of fresh coriander leaves, finely chopped

* Wash the *poha* and place in a strainer to drain.

* Place the oil and onions in a microwave-safe bowl. Add the slit green chillies, curry leaves and crushed peanuts and cook, uncovered, on HIGH (100%) for three minutes.

* Add the turmeric powder, *poha* and salt. Mix well and cook, covered, on HIGH (100%) for five minutes.

* Add the lemon juice, mix well, garnish with chopped coriander leaves and serve hot.

Gur Ki Meethi Kadak Puri

2 cups wholewheat flour (*atta*)

¾ cup grated jaggery

¼ cup pure *ghee* + for frying

a pinch of green cardamom powder (optional)

- Mix the jaggery with three-fourth cup of water in a pan and heat the mixture gently over a very low heat till the jaggery melts completely. Strain.

- Place the wholewheat flour in a bowl and add the green cardamom powder. Rub in the pure *ghee* till the mixture resembles breadcrumbs.

- Add the jaggery mixture and knead into a stiff dough. Cover with a damp cloth and allow the dough to rest for half an hour.

- Divide the dough into sixteen equal portions and shape into balls. Roll out into three-inch *puris* and prick on both sides with a fork.

- Heat *ghee* in a *kadai* and deep-fry the *puris* in moderately hot *ghee* till golden and crisp. Drain on absorbent paper.

- Serve hot or cold.

Cheeley-Poode

2 cups gram flour (*besan*)

½ cup fenugreek leaves (*methi*)

salt to taste

¼ teaspoon turmeric powder

1 teaspoon red chilli powder

½ teaspoon *chaat masala* powder

1 tablespoon lemon juice

1 medium onion, chopped

oil for shallow-frying

1 cup grated cottage cheese (*paneer*)

½ cup grated processed cheese

1 teaspoon red chilli powder

- Combine the *besan*, fenugreek leaves, salt, turmeric powder, red chilli powder, *chaat masala* powder, lemon juice and onion in a bowl. Stir in three-fourth cup of water to make a moderately thick batter.

- Heat a *tawa* and add a little oil. Pour a ladleful of batter and spread it slightly over the *tawa*. Cook over low heat till the *cheeley* is cooked on one side. Drizzle some oil around the sides and over the top.

- Place some grated *paneer* in the centre of the *cheeley*. Sprinkle with grated cheese and chilli powder.

- Fold the two sides over the stuffing and serve hot.

INTERNATIONAL BREAKFASTS

Microwave Oat And Apricot Porridge

1 cup porridge oats

6 ready-to-eat dried apricots, chopped

3½ cups milk

6 stoned prunes, chopped

1½ tablespoons chopped candied ginger

20 almonds, chopped

caster sugar to taste

- Soak the oats in the milk in a microwave-safe bowl for fifteen minutes.

- Cook in a microwave oven on HIGH (100%) for two minutes. Stir well. Cook on HIGH (100%) for another two minutes.

- Add the apricots, prunes, candied ginger and almonds and mix well. Set aside to cool completely.

- Stir in the caster sugar to taste and serve.

Orange And Choco-Chip Muffins

1½ cups refined flour (*maida*)

1 teaspoon chopped orange rind

½ cup orange juice

½ cup chocolate chips

2 teaspoons baking powder

½ teaspoon soda bicarbonate

¾ cup powdered sugar

2 tablespoons cocoa powder

¼ teaspoon salt

¾ cup buttermilk

a few drops of vanilla essence

½ cup butter, melted

- Preheat the oven to 180°C. Grease twelve muffin moulds.

- Sift the flour, baking powder, soda bicarbonate, powdered sugar, cocoa powder and salt into a large bowl and mix well.

- In a separate bowl, mix together the buttermilk, orange rind and vanilla essence. Add the melted butter and whisk well. Add the orange juice and mix again.

- Add the buttermilk mixture to the flour mixture and mix well. Add half the chocolate chips and mix.

- Pour the batter into the prepared muffin moulds and sprinkle the remaining chocolate chips on top. Place the moulds in the oven and bake for twenty to thirty minutes.

- Remove from the oven and leave to stand for about ten minutes. Turn out of the moulds and serve warm.

Triple Decker Sandwich

12 slices day-old bread
1½ cups cream cheese
1 cup cheese spread
a few iceberg lettuce leaves
3-4 cucumbers, peeled and sliced
4 medium potatoes, peeled and sliced

salt to taste
black pepper powder to taste
3-4 tomatoes, sliced
5-6 pickled gherkins, sliced
1 teaspoon crushed red chillies

- Mix the cream cheese and cheese spread together to make a smooth paste.
- Spread a portion of the cheese paste on one slice of bread. Top with a lettuce leaf and cover with a layer of cucumber and potato slices. Sprinkle salt and black pepper powder and cover with another slice of bread.
- Spread a generous portion of the cream cheese paste over the top of the second slice of bread. Top with a few lettuce leaves, followed by tomato slices. Arrange sliced gherkins over the tomato and sprinkle with red chilli flakes.

- Spread a portion of the cream cheese on the third slice and place it over the tomato layer with the cream cheese side facing downwards.
- Cut the triple-layered sandwich diagonally into two triangles and serve immediately.
- Repeat the process for the remaining sandwiches. Serve immediately.

Muesli With Fruit

Basic Muesli

2 cups porridge oats

¼ cup ready-to-eat dried
apricots, chopped

15-20 almonds, sliced

¼ cup black currants

1 cup cornflakes

To Serve

¼ cup dried figs, chopped

fresh fruit such as strawberries,
bananas, apples, grapes, chopped

honey (optional) to taste

cold milk or yogurt

- For the basic muesli, dry-roast the porridge oats. Combine the roasted oats, apricots, almonds, black currants and cornflakes, in a bowl. Store in an airtight container.

- To serve, place a few spoons of muesli into a bowl. Add the chopped figs and chopped fresh fruit. Sweeten with honey if desired. Pour the milk over the muesli and serve. You may heat the milk if desired.

- If serving the muesli with yogurt, add the figs, fresh fruit, honey and yogurt to the muesli. Mix and let stand for about five to ten minutes before serving.

Crunchy Fruit, Yogurt And Cheese

2 large apples, cubed

½ medium muskmelon, cubed

2 large bananas, cubed

2 large pears, cubed

3-4 plums, pitted

2 sweet limes, pith removed, sliced

2-3 tablespoons honey

1½ cups thick yogurt

½ cup cream cheese

2 tablespoons strawberry crush

5-6 sweet biscuits, crushed

8-10 prunes

- Combine the fruit and honey in a bowl.
- Whisk the thick yogurt in a separate bowl. Add the cream cheese and strawberry crush.
- Reserve some crushed biscuits for garnishing and add the rest to the yogurt mixture.
- Partially fill a stemmed glass with the mixed fruit; add a few prunes. Top with the yogurt mixture. Arrange another layer of fruit, topped with yogurt mixture. Garnish with a prune and sprinkle crushed biscuits on top.

Grilled Corn And Capsicum Toasties

8 slices white bread

1 cup sweet corn kernels, boiled

1 medium green capsicum, chopped

1½ cups grated cheese

2-3 green chillies, chopped

2 tablespoons chopped fresh coriander leaves

1 medium onion, chopped

7-8 black peppercorns, crushed

salt to taste

- Preheat the oven to 180°C.
- In a bowl, mix together the sweet corn, capsicum, cheese, green chillies, coriander leaves, onion, crushed peppercorns and salt. Divide the mixture into eight equal portions.
- Toast the slices of bread on one side on a *tawa*.
- Spread the corn and cheese mixture on the other side.
- Place on a baking tray and bake till the topping turns golden brown.
- Cut each slice diagonally in half and serve hot with tomato ketchup.

Spinach And Mushroom Pancakes

Pancakes

¾ cup wholewheat flour (*atta*)

1 cup + 2 tablespoons skimmed milk

salt to taste

¼ teaspoon white pepper powder

¼ teaspoon carom seeds (*ajwain*)

½ teaspoon oil

1 cup grated cheese

2 medium tomatoes, sliced

Stuffing

1 teaspoon oil

1 medium onion, chopped

8-10 fresh button mushrooms, ground coarsely

20-25 large spinach leaves (*palak*), chopped roughly

salt to taste

¼ teaspoon white pepper powder

6-8 garlic cloves, chopped

- To make the stuffing, heat the oil and sauté the onion for thirty seconds. Add the mushrooms and continue to cook till almost dry. Add the spinach and cook till dry.

- Add the salt and white pepper powder to taste, stir in the garlic and remove from heat and keep warm.

- For the batter, place the wholewheat flour in a bowl. Add one cup of milk, salt, white pepper powder and carom seeds. Whisk well to make a smooth batter.

- Heat a six-inch non-stick pan and grease lightly. Pour half a ladleful of batter and spread into a three-inch round with the back of the ladle. Cook for half a minute over medium heat, turn over and cook for a few seconds.

- Spread a portion of cooked spinach on three-fourths of each pancake.

- Spread some of the grated cheese and top with some tomato slices. Fold it ensuring that the filling does not spill out. Make the rest of the pancakes. Use three-fourth cup of grated cheese in the filling.

- Preheat the oven to 225ºC.

- Place the pancakes in a baking dish, sprinkle with remaining grated cheese and two tablespoons of skimmed milk. Bake till the cheese melts.

- Serve immediately.

Manchurian Rolls

4 crusty bread rolls

1 medium cabbage, grated

1 medium carrot, grated

¼ small cauliflower, grated

salt to taste

3 medium spring onions with greens, chopped

¼ cup refined flour (*maida*)

¼ cup cornflour

oil for deep-frying

Sauce

2 tablespoons oil

1 inch fresh ginger, chopped

4-6 garlic cloves, chopped

2-inch celery stalk, chopped

3 green chillies, chopped

2 tablespoons light soy sauce

1 teaspoon sugar

¼ teaspoon MSG (optional)

salt to taste

1 cup vegetable stock

2 tablespoons cornflour

1 tablespoon white vinegar

- Mix the cabbage, carrot and cauliflower in a bowl and thoroughly rub in one teaspoon of salt. Add the spring onions, refined flour and cornflour and mix thoroughly. Shape into lemon-sized balls.

- Heat the oil in a wok and deep-fry the vegetable balls over medium heat in small batches for three or four minutes or until golden brown. Drain on absorbent paper.

- Heat two tablespoons of oil in a wok or a pan and stir-fry the ginger and garlic for one minute. Add the celery and green chillies and stir-fry for one minute longer.

- Add the soy sauce, sugar, MSG and salt to taste. Stir in the vegetable stock and bring to a boil.

- Mix two tablespoons of cornflour with half a cup of water and stir into the hot stock. Cook, stirring continuously, for a couple of minutes, or until the sauce starts to thicken.

- Add the fried vegetable balls and vinegar and mix well.

- Split the rolls once. Stuff the vegetable balls and sauce into each one. Serve immediately.

Breakfast Wrap

4 tortillas

2 teaspoons olive oil

1 large onion, chopped

1 large green capsicum, seeded and diced

¼ small red or green cabbage, shredded (optional)

Salt to taste

black pepper powder to taste

1 cup grated tofu

2 tablespoons Tabasco sauce

½ tablespoons to tomato ketchup

1 tablespoon chopped fresh parsley

½ cup grated cheese

- Heat the olive oil in a non-stick pan and sauté the onion, green capsicum and cabbage till tender.

- Add salt and black pepper powder to taste and mix.

- Add the tofu, Tabasco sauce and parsley. Mix and cook over high heat, stirring continuously, until the tofu is firm and heated through.

- Place one-fourth of this filling on each tortilla. Sprinkle one-fourth of the grated cheese. Roll the tortilla up and serve immediately.

Power-Packed Bowl

1 medium orange

8 cherry tomatoes, halved

2 slices fresh pineapple, cut into ½-inch cubes

1 medium ripe mango, cut into ½-inch cubes

1 small apple, cut into ½-inch cubes

1 peach (optional), cut into ½-inch cubes

6 ready-to-eat dried apricots

100 grams cottage cheese (*paneer*), cut into ½-inch cubes

1 cup bean sprouts

6 lettuce leaves, sliced fine

Dressing

4 tablespoons olive oil

1 tablespoon balsamic vinegar

salt to taste

5-6 black peppercorns, freshly ground

2 tablespoons fresh orange juice

- Separate orange segments, remove pips and slice them.
- Place the orange, cherry tomatoes, pineapple, mango, apple, peach, dried apricots and *paneer* in a deep bowl. Add bean sprouts and toss to mix.
- For the dressing, mix together the olive oil, balsamic vinegar, salt, freshly ground black peppercorns and fresh orange juice. Mix well and chill till required. Just before serving, add shredded lettuce and dressing to fruit and bean sprout mixture and serve immediately.

Garden Vegetable Rolls

8 lettuce leaves, roughly torn

2 large tomatoes, thinly sliced

2 large cucumbers, thinly sliced

4 wholewheat hot dog rolls

2 tablespoons butter

2 tablespoons mustard paste

8-10 black peppercorns, freshly ground

salt to taste

Thousand Island Dressing

4 tablespoons eggless mayonnaise

1 tablespoon tomato ketchup

1 teaspoon Tabasco sauce

1 jalapeño chilli, chopped

1 pickled onion, chopped

1 pickled gherkin, chopped

- To prepare the Thousand Island dressing mix all the ingredients well.
- Slit the buns without cutting through. Spread a little butter on both sides.
- Arrange the lettuce, cucumber and tomato slices evenly on one half of each roll. Sprinkle a little salt and ground peppercorns.
- Drizzle a little mustard paste and Thousand Island dressing. Cover with the second half and serve immediately.

Potato And Pasta Hash Browns

5 medium potatoes, parboiled

1 cup macaroni, blanched

3 tablespoons butter

1 medium onion, chopped

salt to taste

10-12 black peppercorns, coarsely ground

a pinch of nutmeg powder

2 tablespoons chopped fresh parsley

- Cool, peel and grate the parboiled potatoes.
- Heat two tablespoons of butter in a pan; add the onion and sauté till translucent. Remove from heat.
- Preheat the oven to 200°C.
- Mix the potatoes, macaroni and onion together with salt, half a teaspoon of ground peppercorns, nutmeg powder and parsley.
- Mix well and spread the potato mixture in a greased baking tray.
- Dot with the remaining butter and sprinkle with the remaining ground peppercorns.
- Bake for ten to fifteen minutes, or till the top turns a light golden brown.
- Serve hot.

Fruity Yogurt With Cereal Topping

2 ripe mangoes, peeled and cubed

2 medium apples, cubed

8-10 cherries, stoned

1½ cups yogurt, whisked

2 tablespoons sugar

1 teaspoon raisins (*kishmish*)

3-4 cashew nuts, chopped

3 tablespoons muesli, toasted

- Combine the mangoes, apples and cherries and refrigerate until ready to serve.
- In a bowl, combine the yogurt and sugar and whisk until the sugar dissolves completely.
- Just before serving, mix in the chilled fruit, raisins and cashew nuts.
- Spoon into individual bowls, sprinkle the toasted muesli over and serve at once.

Saucy Vegetable And Baked Bean Hot Rolls

4 hot dog rolls

2 tablespoons butter

4-5 baby corn cobs, chopped

4-5 fresh button mushrooms, quartered

1 cup baked beans

3 tablespoons tomato-chilli sauce

salt to taste

4 lettuce leaves

8 tablespoons grated cheese

mustard sauce as required

- Heat a *tawa*. Slit the hot dog rolls without cutting through and roast them on the *tawa* using one tablespoon of melted butter. Remove when done and set aside.

- Heat the remaining tablespoon of butter in a non-stick pan and sauté the baby corn and button mushrooms for two minutes. Add the baked beans, tomato-chilli sauce and salt. Divide into four portions.

- Place one lettuce leaf in each hot dog roll. Fill with one portion of bean filling. Cover generously with two tablespoons of cheese. Drizzle with mustard sauce and serve immediately.

BEVERAGES

Masala Chai

4-6 teaspoons tea leaves

1 cup milk

1 teaspoon *chai masala*

4 teaspoons sugar

- Boil three cups of water in a pan. Add the tea leaves, milk, *chai masala* and sugar and bring the mixture to a boil again. Boil for a couple of minutes.
- Strain and serve piping hot.

Chai Masala

Dry-roast and grind to a fine powder 1 inch cinnamon, 4 green cardamoms, 16 black peppercorns and ¼ teaspoon grated nutmeg. Sift the powder and store in an airtight container.

Filter Coffee

3 tablespoons freshly ground
coffee powder

2 tablespoons sugar

4 cups milk

- Bring one cup of water to a boil in a pan.
- Add the coffee powder in the upper chamber of a filter-coffee maker.
- Pour the boiling water over the coffee; cover and set aside to let the water filter through the powder.
- Heat the milk till boiling. Pour the milk into four cups and add sugar to taste.
- Pour the coffee decoction into the cups and stir. Serve at once.

Power Punch

1 kilogram carrots	8-10 ice cubes
500 grams beetroot	black salt to taste
4 oranges	orange rind, cut into thin strips

- Pass the carrots, beetroots and oranges through a juicer and collect the juice.
- Pour the juices into a blender; add ice cubes and black salt.
- Blend for a minute and pour into tall glasses.
- Decorate with strips of orange rind if desired.

Melon And Mango Smoothie

BEVERAGES

1 medium-sized ripe musk melon

2 ripe Alphonso mangoes

2 tablespoons strawberry crush

1 cup crushed ice

- Cut the melon into wedges, peel and remove seeds. Chop half a wedge into half-inch cubes. Chop the remaining melon into one-inch cubes. Place in a freezer for an hour.

- Peel the mangoes and chop one slice into half-inch cubes. Chop the remaining mango into one-inch cubes. Place in a freezer for one hour.

- Place the large cubes of melon and mango in a blender with the strawberry crush and one cup of crushed ice. Blend till smooth and frothy.

- Pour into individual glasses and serve, topped with the smaller melon and mango cubes.

Badam Doodh

60 almonds

8 cups milk

a generous pinch of saffron

½ teaspoon green cardamom powder

a pinch of nutmeg powder

12 tablespoons sugar

- Blanch and peel the almonds. Slice fifteen almonds and grind the rest to a paste.
- Bring the milk to a boil in a thick-bottomed pan. Lower heat, add the almond paste and simmer for fifteen to twenty minutes.
- Add the saffron, cardamom powder, nutmeg powder and sugar and mix well.
- Pour into individual glasses, garnish with sliced almonds and serve hot.

Banana and Fig Milk Shake

3 ripe bananas, peeled and chopped

12 dried figs (*anjeer*), soaked and chopped

3½ cups chilled milk

2 tablespoons sugar

2 tablespoons honey

crushed ice

- Process the banana, figs and half the milk in a blender.
- Add the sugar, honey and the remaining milk and process again.
- Add the ice and blend again.
- Pour into individual glasses and serve immediately.

Honey And Fruit Smoothie

5 tablespoons honey

3 ripe bananas, peeled and chopped

2 ripe mangoes, peeled and chopped

2 tablespoons lemon juice

2 cups yogurt

8-10 ice cubes, crushed

fresh mint sprigs, to decorate

- Place the banana and mango pieces in the freezer for one hour.
- Place the frozen fruit, honey, lemon juice and yogurt in a blender and blend until smooth.
- Add the crushed ice cubes and blend again.
- Pour into individual glasses and serve, garnished with mint sprigs.

Carrot and Tomato Smoothie

8 medium carrots

12 medium tomatoes

1 celery stalk, chopped

salt to taste

1 teaspoon black pepper powder

ice cubes as required

4 tablespoons lemon juice

- Chop the carrots into one-inch cubes and tomatoes into quarters. Place in the freezer till completely frozen.
- Place the frozen tomatoes in a blender and process for a few seconds. Add the frozen carrot and blend again.
- Add the celery, salt and pepper powder and continue to blend.
- Add the ice cubes and lemon juice and blend till well-mixed.
- Serve chilled.

Pineapple Power Drink

4 cups tinned pineapple juice

1 tinned pineapple ring, chopped

1 tablespoon honey

½ inch ginger, chopped

1 cup crushed ice

- Place all the ingredients in a blender with two cups of cold water. Blend on medium speed till smooth.
- Add the crushed ice and serve, chilled in tall glasses.

Strawberry And Orange Soya Shake

4 tablespoons strawberry crush

1 orange

4 cups chilled soya milk

4 teaspoons sugar

4 scoops vanilla ice cream

6 tablespoons orange squash

2 cups crushed ice

- Peel and remove the pith from the orange segments. Peel off the white membrane and separate the flakes. Place in a refrigerator to chill for ten minutes.

- Place the strawberry crush, soya milk, sugar, vanilla ice cream and orange squash in a blender and blend till smooth.

- Place the crushed ice in four glasses. Pour the strawberry-soya shake over the ice.

- Top with the orange flakes and serve immediately.